D1179128

Medicine in the Industrial World

John D. Clare

WAYLAND

First published in 2006 by Hodder Wayland,
an imprint of Hodder Children's Books

Reprinted in 2007 by Wayland, an imprint of Hachette Children's Books

© Wayland 2006

Commissioning editor: Victoria Brooker
Editor: Hayley Leach
Inside design: Peta Morey
Cover design: Hodder Wayland
Consultant: Dr Robert Arnott, University of Birmingham Medical School

British Library Cataloguing in Publication Data:

Clare, John D., 1952-
The industrial world. - (The history of medicine; v. 5)
1.Medicine - History - 19th century - Juvenile literature
2.Medicine, Ancient - Juvenile literature
I.Title
610.9'034

ISBN-13: 978 0 7502 4642 2

Printed and bound in China

Hachette Children's Books
338 Euston Road, London NW1 3BH

Picture Acknowledgements. The author and Publisher would like to thank the
following for allowing their pictures to be reproduced in this publication:
The Advertising Archives 53; AFP/Getty Images 24; akg-images 8; Archives
Charmet/Bridgeman Art Library 15 and title page; The Art Archive/British
Museum/Eileen Tweedy 38; The Art Archive/Tate Gallery London/Eileen Tweedy 56;
John Bavosi/Science PhotoLibrary 43; Chris Beetles, London, U.K./Bridgeman Art
Library 47; Bettmann/Corbis 8, 17, 25, 29, 32, 34, 35, 40 and cover, 49, 55 and
index page, 57, 58; Bibliotheque des Arts Decoratifs, Paris, France, Archives
Charmet/Bridgeman Art Library 59; Stanley B. Burns, MD and the Burns Archive
NY/Science Photo Library 41; Burstein Collection/Corbis 54; Patrice
Cartier/Bridgeman Art Library 39; Jean-Loup Charmet/Science Photo Library 7, 14;
Corbis 19, 36, 37; Getty Images 5, 19; Historical Picture Archive/Corbis 48
(bottom); Hulton-Deutsch Collection/Corbis 33; Mary Evans Picture Library 23;
New-York Historical Society, New York, USA/Bridgeman Art Library 51; Roger
Ressmeyer/Corbis 16; Science Photo Library 21, 26, 42, 48 (top); Barbara
Singer/Bridgeman Art Library 45; Time Life Pictures/Getty Images 52; Wellcome
Library, London 4, 6, 10, 11 and 60, 12, 13, 20, 22, 28, 27, 30, 44, 46

Contents

Chapter 1

The world of 1800-1914

Creating a problem

The nineteenth century saw the coming of the Industrial Revolution – particularly in Britain, France, Germany and America – and the changes it brought altered the face of medicine for ever.

Working in the new factories and mines led to a whole range of occupational diseases – such as cancers, poisoning, lung diseases and dermatitis – as well as new, horrific machine injuries. The rapidly-growing cities swamped existing systems for dealing with refuse and sewage, and caused 'filth' diseases such as typhus (a disease passed on by lice), tuberculosis and cholera. Acute infectious diseases such as whooping cough and scarlet fever swept through populations crowded together in the urban slums. At the same time there were increases in social diseases such as alcoholism and syphilis, and the American psychiatrist Amariah Brigham (1798–1849) attributed the growth of mental breakdowns and 'nervous diseases' to the stress and hectic pace of industrial life.

Traders and empire-builders travelled to different parts of the world encountering a range of new diseases – for instance yellow fever and malaria – that sometimes simply killed them outright or which they introduced to their home countries.

William Hogarth's *Consultation of Physicians* (1736) is sometimes called *The Company of Undertakers*, presumably because Hogarth was suggesting that the doctors actually killed their patients. A group of doctors study a urine flask. They sniff posies in the end of their sticks because they think this will prevent them getting disease.

The eighteenth-century doctor

Facing these new forces of disease was a medical profession utterly inadequate to the task. In 1800, although some doctors were influential members of society and friends of the rich and powerful, most struggled to make a living, and had to supplement their income by farming or land deals. In the United States, after the American Revolution, there were so few doctors that clergymen often doubled up as physicians.

Eighteenth century doctors made house calls on the wealthy, with all the tools of their profession in a single bag. Relationships were personal and – although they knew about anatomy and could recognise a range of diseases – their chief function was to reassure. They had a number of medicaments and drugs to alleviate the symptoms of the illnesses they commonly encountered, but they were largely powerless to cure disease. Some of their cures were so unpleasant and harmful that the American poet and doctor Oliver Wendell Holmes (1809–1894) suggested that if all medicines were sunk to the bottom of the ocean 'it would be all the better for mankind – and all the worse for the fishes'.

The famous American doctor Benjamin Rush (1745–1813) – sometimes called the 'Father of American medicine' – was one of the men who signed the American Declaration of Independence. He advocated 'bleeding to the limit of endurance'. The British writer William Cobbett said that Rush's cure was 'one of those great discoveries which have contributed to the depopulation of the earth'.

Heroes of health?

Historians have taken two approaches to the study of the history of medicine. Until recently, medical historians tended to emphasise the scientific developments of medicine, and their accounts viewed medical progress as the result of advances made by remarkable individuals – the so-called 'heroes of health'. More recently, however, historians have chosen to stress the wider underlying social and economic developments. This is called the social history of medicine.

The cholera epidemic of 1831-2

In 1817, a virulent form of cholera broke out in Jessore, near Calcutta in India. From there it passed to Bombay (1818) and thence, six years later, spread through Persia – despite the guns that villagers fired to try and frighten it away. When it reached Russia in 1830, the government tried blockading infected villages using troops. The strategy did not work: the disease travelled into Sweden, where strict quarantine rules also failed to stop it spreading.

Meanwhile, a ship from Cairo brought cholera to mainland Europe in 1831. Spain introduced the death penalty for bringing cholera into the country. In Hungary, mobs accused the rich people of poisoning the wells. In Germany, beggars who claimed to be infected promised to go away if they were paid. In Paris, the first victim dropped dead during a masked ball, sparking a panic evacuation to the countryside.

The *Sunderland Herald* of 1831 described the symptoms of cholera as: 'Vomiting or purging of a liquid like rice-water...the face becomes sharp and shrunken, the eyes sink and look wild, the lips, face, neck, hands and feet, and the whole surface of the body is leaden, blue, purple, black...The skin is deadly cold, the tongue flabby and chilled like a piece of dead flesh. The respiration is often quick but irregular...In the treatment of this disease it is necessary to state that no specific remedy has yet been discovered.'

THE APPEARANCE AFTER DEATH OF A VICTIM TO THE INDIAN CHOLERA
WHO DIED AT SUNDERLAND

In October 1831, the first reported case of cholera occurred in Sunderland, England. Over the next two years it killed nearly 22,000 people in Britain. If the Americans had hoped that the Atlantic would prove an insuperable barrier, they were mistaken. In 1832, a

boatload of Irish immigrants took the disease to
Montréal in Canada, from there it worked its way down
to New York, causing a flight of inhabitants wherever it
went, which in turn spread the disease further.

Endemic diseases

Cholera made people panic and, as a result, it was one
of the main reasons why governments sought to make
advances in public health. But many nineteenth
century diseases were more deadly than cholera. In
Britain, in the years 1848–55 (years which included
two cholera epidemics), cholera was responsible for
only 83,000 deaths (2.7 per cent). During this time,
endemic diseases such as tuberculosis (12 per cent of
deaths), pneumonia (5 per cent of deaths), typhus (4
per cent of deaths) and scarlet fever (4 per cent of
deaths) were much bigger killers.

The bacillus *vibrio cholerae*
(a germ transmitted in the
faeces of humans) is common
and normally benign. In 1996,
US researchers discovered,
however, that the cholera toxin
is carried by a virus, and when
this virus infects *vibrio
cholerae* the resultant strain is
virulent. There were renewed
pandemics in 1849 and 1866.
This illustration, still showing
cholera as the 'grim reaper', is
from a French magazine of
December 1912.

King cholera

The cholera epidemic of
1831–1832 gives us an insight
into how effective the medicine
of the nineteenth century was.
Cholera arrived suddenly and
killed quickly and horribly.
Although it afflicted primarily the
poor and the weak, it killed the
wealthy and the strong just as
effectively. Suggested therapies
included immense dosages of
laudanum (opium), rubbing the
body with mustard, tobacco
smoke enemas, electric shock
therapy, and oilcloth plugs forced
into the rectum to stop the
diarrhoea. Nothing worked.
Cholera demonstrated the
powerlessness of humankind in the face
of disease in the nineteenth century.

LE CHOLÉRA

The means to a solution

Although it created many medical problems, the Industrial Revolution also stimulated great advances in technology and science. Improvements in machine tools and mechanical engineering led to new medical instruments and machines as well as railway trains and factory machinery. Improved communications, such as photographs, the telegraph and the wireless, helped new medical knowledge to be shared and applied all over the world.

It was not just that medicine had access to new chemicals and machines – though both were to revolutionise medicine by the end of the nineteenth century. The change in attitudes and beliefs that came with the Industrial Revolution also created a culture in which medical discoveries were possible. New political theories such as democracy and socialism – stressing as they did the rights of ordinary people – led ordinary people to demand access to health. Changing ideas about the role and abilities of women led to women doctors, and a revolution in nursing. The ideas of Charles Darwin about evolution (1859) and of Gregor Mendel about genes and heredity (1869) changed what people thought about the nature of life and disease.

The front page of Darwin's *The Origin of Species* (1859). Darwin's ideas about evolution helped to change attitudes to medicine. People started to reason that if humankind was not God's special creation, perhaps doctors had a right to affect the nature of life.

ON

THE ORIGIN OF SPECIES

BY MEANS OF NATURAL SELECTION,

OR THE

PRESERVATION OF FAVOURED RACES IN THE STRUGGLE
FOR LIFE.

By CHARLES DARWIN, M.A.,

FELLOW OF THE ROYAL, GEOLOGICAL, LINNÆAN, ETC., SOCIETIES;
AUTHOR OF 'JOURNAL OF RESEARCHES DURING H. M. S. BEAGLE'S VOYAGE
ROUND THE WORLD.'

LONDON:
JOHN MURRAY, ALBEMARLE STREET.
1859.
P. 2:5.

The right of Translation is reserved.

Eugenics

The new ideas of evolution and genes led the English explorer and scientist Francis Galton (1822–1911) to develop the theory that intelligence – and certain physical and mental defects – are hereditary. Although it reached its most wicked conclusion in Nazi Germany, the idea of 'eugenics' (from the Greek meaning 'well-born') was taken up in America in the nineteenth century. There, Richard Dugdale's study of a New York family of paupers and criminals, *The Jukes* (1875), led a number of states to try to stop these 'defects' from being passed to the next generation. They made laws for the compulsory sterilization of the 'feebleminded, insane, criminalistic, inebriate, diseased, blind, deaf, deformed and dependent'.

Nationalism and war

Nationalism (the belief that one's own nation is superior to all others) – a powerful ideology in the nineteenth century – stimulated further medical advances. French and German researchers competed to make the more significant discoveries; the rivalry between Frenchman Louis Pasteur and the German Robert Koch (see Chapter 3) was particularly intense. The need to care for armies in time of war stimulated significant developments in medical organization, nursing, hygiene and surgery, which then had 'spin-offs' into medical care at home. As the nations scrambled to build up their empires, they developed medicine to combat tropical diseases, not to help the people who lived there (who were often immune), but to protect their soldiers and administrators from illness.

Medicine and war: an amputation in the field during the American Civil War.

Chapter 2

How did knowledge about the body improve?

A shortage of bodies

Well before the beginning of the nineteenth century, the Scottish obstetrician William Hunter (1718–1783) had established the need to learn anatomy by dissection. By 1823, there were 1,000 medical students studying anatomy in London alone, and anatomy had become a normal part of a doctor's training – the Czech anatomist Karel Rokitanski (1804-1878) reputedly conducted 60,000 dissections.

Since doctors were only allowed to dissect the bodies of executed murderers, however, there was a severe shortage of bodies, and for many years this shortage was met, notably in Britain and America, by 'resurrection men' (grave-robbers). The answer, of

The most famous 'resurrectionists' were the Irishmen William Burke and William Hare. Hare ran a lodging house in Edinburgh. When an old soldier died owing him money, Hare sold the body to a Dr Knox for £7 10s – more than the original debt. Sensing easy money, Hare and one of his lodgers, Burke, then began suffocating lodgers and selling the bodies. They were eventually caught, and Burke was hanged.

course, was to sanction more dissections, and in Britain the Anatomy Act of 1832 allowed doctors to dissect any body, providing the relatives agreed. The American state of Massachusetts had passed a similar act the previous year, and other US states followed, although grave robbing for dissection continued in some American states up to 1900.

The popularisation of anatomy

Historians believe that during the nineteenth century, people in Britain and America learned to think of themselves as 'anatomical beings'. Doctors lectured artists in anatomy, and put on slide shows for the public. After the 1870s, anatomy became part of the school curriculum for both primary and secondary school pupils.

Applying technology

Although the microscope had been invented in the seventeenth century, it was no good for detailed work, because the single lens caused distortion and 'rainbow' fringes round the edges. In 1826, Joseph Jackson Lister (father of the famous surgeon, see Chapter 5) invented a system of multiple spaced lenses which corrected the problem, and this, for the first time, allowed doctors to study the cells of animals. This invention led to the science of histology (the study of tissues to diagnose disease).

189.—Surgical Anatomy of the Arteries of the Neck. Right Side.

In 1858, the Scottish anatomist Henry Gray wrote *Gray's Anatomy*, an anatomy textbook organized by systems – bones, joints, muscles, cardio-vascular systems etc. The 1918 edition had 1,247 engravings, many in colour. It became hugely popular in both Britain and America, and not just as a textbook for students and surgeons: many families bought their own private copy, and today it is available for free in its entirety on the Internet.

Frankenstein

Mary Shelley's novel, *Frankenstein* (first edition 1818, third edition 1831), shows people's doubts about anatomy at the time. In the novel, Victor Frankenstein is an anatomical surgeon. He assembles the body parts for his monster by robbing graves, but eventually becomes implicated in murder as a means of getting the required body parts.

The Paris school

The French Revolution changed medicine. The theory of 'the rights of man', upon which the Revolution was based, included the right to health care. In 1794, the new government set up three important centres of research known as *écoles de santé* (schools of health). One of the principles of the Revolution was equality, and students of any background were admitted to these centres by open examination. At the same time, the Revolution overthrew the traditional medical authorities and allowed medical practitioners more freedom. As a result, French medicine made significant advances and the Paris hospitals became centres of medical research.

In 1816, the French doctor, René Laënnec, invented the stethoscope. Doctors learned to tap the patient's chest, and to interpret the different sounds produced: auscultation. Laënnec's book, *Traité de l'auscultation mediate* (*Dissertation on indirect auscultation*), explained in detail what doctors ought to listen for, and – until X-rays – auscultation became the main method of internal diagnosis.

Clinical medicine and the beginnings of physiology

One of the most influential Paris doctors was Pierre Louis. His book, *Essay on Clinical Instruction* (1834), suggested that symptoms (the outward result of the illness) were poor indicators of disease. What doctors should look for, he argued, were 'signs' (the changes and processes going on *inside* the body). His ideas mark the start of clinical medicine, whereby doctors diagnosed diseases on the basis of a detailed physical examination. Having diagnosed what they thought was the disease, after the patient had died, the Paris doctors then dissected the patient to prove that their diagnosis had been correct.

Just as important was the French doctor Francois Broussais (1772–1838) who argued that there was nothing particularly different about disease. There was, he said, a continuum from health to disease, and illness occurred simply when the normal functioning of the body went wrong. Doctors started to study physiology: the normal functioning of the body. Following on from Broussais, the French physiologist Claude Bernard (1813–1878) studied the digestive system and developed the idea of 'homeostatis' – the theory that the body is a series of systems designed to keep itself in balance, even if external conditions change. Bernard argued that physiology could only be studied in the laboratory, by animal experiments and vivisection.

One of the most influential American doctors, pictured here, was William Henry Welch (1850–1934). The ideas of the 'Paris School' of doctors changed the international practice of medicine – they mark the beginning of modern medicine – and students from Britain and America flocked to be taught in France and Germany. Welch studied in Germany but returned to America to run the new medical department at John Hopkins University (1884), where he insisted on European standards of scientific study and clinical laboratory work.

Experimental physiology

In 1836, the Czech physiologist Jan Purkinje – who was the first person to study brain cells under the microscope – published a memo in which he argued that physiology was a separate discipline, and that funding was needed for physiology institutes and laboratories. His ideas can be said to mark the beginning of 'experimental physiology' (investigating how the body works).

Reductionism and the first physiologists

In 1847, a group of German physiologists declared that
the processes of the human body were merely chemical
reactions, no different to those found in the world of
inorganic chemistry. This idea was known as
'reductionism'.

As a result, researchers began to measure and
experiment on the body, and made great advances in
understanding how the body works. In Germany,
Hermann von Helmholtz measured the speed of
electronic impulses along the nerves (1848). In Russia,
Ivan Pavlov, in a famous experiment, showed that reflex
responses (e.g. salivating when a dinner gong sounded)
could be learned (1890s). In England, in 1902, Ernest
Starling and William Bayliss discovered secretin (which
stimulates the stomach to produce digestive juices), the
first of many hormones to be discovered. In 1912,
Casimir Funk, a Polish biochemist, discovered vitamins.
After 1915, doctors identified several diseases which
were caused by vitamin-deficiencies and were curable
using extracts from certain foods.

In 1825, the German scientist
Justus von Liebig (famous for
his work on phosphate
fertilisers, and as the inventor
of Oxo) became Professor of
Chemistry at the University of
Giessen, in the German state
of Hesse. Here, he encouraged
his students to study the
chemistry of different
metabolic processes. In 1828,
his co-researcher, Freidrich
Wöhler, synthesised urea (pure
urine), thus proving that the
compounds in the human body
were no different from other
inorganic chemicals.

Medical machines

As part of these scientific experiments, researchers invented machines to measure the workings of the body. Carl Ludwig invented the kymograph (1847) to monitor the pulse. Wilhelm Röntgen invented X-rays (1895). And Willem Einthoven developed the electrocardiograph (*c.* 1900), which measured the electrical activity of the heart.

Where before, patients might have been described in general terms, such as 'feverish', now they were scientifically and statistically monitored. By the end of the century, doctors understood the human body as never before.

X-rays are an example of how advances in science and industry were applied to medicine. This first X-ray was of Röntgen's wife's hand, including her wedding ring. The first medical use of X-rays occurred in Liverpool in 1896, when the surgeon Robert Jones used X-rays to remove an air gun pellet from a boy's wrist.

Knowledge of the digestive system

A case from America highlights the enthusiasm of nineteenth century doctors for physiology. Alexis St Martin was a Canadian 'voyageur' (porter and canoe-man) who, in 1822, was shot at point-blank range by a shotgun. Against all expectations, Alexis recovered, but his body, in healing, left a fistula (a hole) right through into his stomach. For the rest of his life, unless this hole was plugged with wadding, half-digested food oozed out continually.

Dr William Beaumont, the American army surgeon who treated Alexis, was so fascinated that he took Alexis to live with him, and spent three years studying the operation of his stomach – mainly by shoving food into the hole on a rope and pulling it out again later to see what had happened to it. Most doctors today are agreed that Beaumont's conduct was thoroughly unethical, but he and St Martin substantially added to our knowledge of the digestive system.

Cell theory

Until the eighteenth century, doctors believed that the body was composed of four 'humours', and that these four liquids (blood, phlegm, and yellow and black bile) determined the state of a person's health. Historians call this 'humoral pathology'.

By the start of the nineteenth century, the Paris school of doctors had begun to question this idea, suggesting that the seat of disease lay in the tissues, not in the so-called 'humours'. The invention of the achromatic lens by Joseph Jackson Lister (see page 11) was to destroy it altogether. In 1839, using the new microscope, the German physiologist Theodor Schwann produced his book *Mikroskopische Untersuchungen* (*Microscopic Researches*) in which he showed that all animal tissues were composed of cells, not humours.

Below is a picture taken with a microscope of brain tissue full of malignant cancer cells.

Rudolph Virchow looking through a magnifying glass. Virchow's skill in communicating his ideas is one of the reasons for his huge influence in the history of medicine.

Rudolf Virchow

Rudolf Virchow (1821–1902) was Professor of Pathological Anatomy in Berlin. He was a reductionist who believed that the body 'follows the ordinary physical and chemical laws'.

In 1858, Virchow published his book *Cellular Pathology* in which he proved that cells controlled all bodily events, from fertilisation and growth to the formation of pus in wounds. Disease, he claimed, was the result of the abnormal development and reproduction of certain cells. This idea, he boasted correctly, marked the death of humoral pathology, and the study of disease at cell level turned out to be the foundation for the developments in curative medicine during the twentieth century.

Cancer

Virchow was especially interested in cancer. In the 1840s, he had described one of the earliest cases of leukemia and went on to make many more studies of tumours. He showed how cancer-tumours grow from cells that have mutated, but then multiply out-of-control. He suggested that cancer was caused by the body's own immune system working on areas of inflammation – an understanding which has become a key idea in the battle against cancer today.

Chapter 3

How did knowledge about disease increase?

Inoculating for smallpox

Smallpox was a terrible disease, which disfigured its victims with ugly 'pock-marks' and, in its most virulent form, killed one in three people who caught it (particularly the weak, poor, old and very young).

Inoculation against smallpox was first developed by the Chinese (*c.* 1000 AD). Using pus from a pock of the less virulent form of the disease, and smearing it on a thread of cloth – so that the virus was greatly attenuated (weakened) – they then infected a person, perhaps by a scratch on the skin. The patient fell ill with a mild case of smallpox, but usually recovered, and was immune thereafter. This procedure was called 'variolation'. Lady Montagu Wortley, wife of the British Ambassador to Turkey, brought the idea of variolation back to Britain in 1721, and the American doctor James Kilpatrick introduced it into South Carolina in the year 1738.

The English doctor Robert Sutton improved the method of variolation by insisting that the patient was rested and well-fed before they were inoculated, but infecting people with the live smallpox virus remained a very dangerous (and sometimes fatal) way of making people immune.

Cowpox and vaccination

Cowpox was a disease similar to smallpox, but it was mild and non-fatal. Farmers knew from experience that people who had caught cowpox never fell ill with smallpox, and a Dorset doctor called Benjamin Jesty had been giving his patients cowpox since 1774. In 1796, when a Gloucestershire girl called Sarah Nelmes caught cowpox, a local doctor, Edward Jenner, used pus from one of

Vaccination against smallpox spread all over the world. It was made compulsory in Germany in 1835, and in Britain in 1853. In 1977, Ali Maow Maalin, a smallpox vaccinator in Somalia, contracted *variola minor* but recovered from the disease. He had the last case of smallpox in the world, and in 1980 the World Health Organisation officially declared the smallpox virus extinct. There are, however, still laboratories where smallpox germs are kept alive, to be used for vaccination.

the pocks on her finger to infect an eight-year-old boy called James Phipps. James caught cowpox, but recovered. A month later, Jenner tried (a number of times) to inoculate him with smallpox, but failed – James Phipps was immune to smallpox.

Was Jenner important in the history of medicine?

His method only provided immunity from one disease and – because no one had a clue *why* it worked until 80 years later – it gave doctors no clues about how to advance further. In fact, since it used a similar disease and not an attenuated (weakened) form of the actual disease, it was not *real* inoculation. It actually pointed doctors in the wrong direction; there were no other illnesses as closely-related as smallpox and cowpox. It is arguable that Jenner's discovery was a lucky co-incidence, and not a step in the progress of medicine.

The word vaccination was taken from the Latin word 'vacca', meaning cow. Pasteur (see page 26) called it vaccination in honour of Jenner's work on the cowpox vaccine. Vaccination was not immediately accepted. There was a popular belief that it would turn people into cows. The Royal Society criticised Jenner, and he had to publish *An Inquiry into the Causes and Effects of the Variolae Vaccinae* (1798) at his own expense so that his ideas would become known.

What causes disease?

The Greeks taught (and doctors until the eighteenth century believed) that disease was caused by an 'imbalance of the humours' (see page 16). During the eighteenth century, belief in the four humours died out, and doctors instead came to think that disease was caused by 'miasmas' (bad smells). For example, the word 'malaria' means, literally, 'bad air'. This idea has a basis in common sense: bad smells are closely associated both with disease and with the unsanitary conditions that cause disease. The 'poisonous miasma' theory of disease persisted well into the nineteenth century and was responsible for many significant advances in public health (see Chapter 4).

Eighteenth century doctors thought that bacteria were the result of disease, not its cause, and they developed the theory of 'spontaneous generation' (the idea that the disease created the bacteria). As late as 1860, the French scientist Felix Pouchet conducted experiments, using the equipment shown, which supposedly 'proved' this theory. Pouchet heated the matter to kill all existing bacteria, then he opened the jars to the air and the matter decomposed, whereupon bacteria 'spontaneously' developed. However, as Pasteur proved, it was the air which carried the bacteria.

Bad smells

Most doctors in the early nineteenth century accepted the idea that foul air caused disease. French doctors compiled a 'smell map' of Paris, to chart the medical geography of the city. One British workman was assured that his family had fallen ill because of his 'remarkably offensive' breath and sweat! In 1855, *The Lancet* claimed that, not only did smelly gases cause disease, but they were also responsible for 'failing strength, flabby muscles, pallid cheeks, lassitude of body and torpidity of mind'.

Doubts about miasmas

After 1800, however, an increasing number of doctors expressed doubts about the 'foul air' theory of disease. They blamed 'zymes' (harmful agents), which might be chemicals, fungi, parasites, or cells from another sick person's body. In 1839, the German physician Johann Schönlein discovered that the itchy skin disease

This 1866 French cartoon of death giving people water from a pump shows that people had realized that infected drinking water caused cholera. In 1854, the English doctor John Snow had proved through meticulous research that cholera cases originated from a single water source, and he stopped the epidemic by taking the handle off the pump – thus proving beyond doubt that cholera was caused, not by a miasma, but by a water-borne impurity.

ringworm was caused by a parasite and, in the 1850s, the English epidemiologist William Budd proved that typhoid was spread by an unknown agent on the faeces of people infected with the disease. Then, in 1855, the German Professor of Public Health, Max von Pettenkofer, suggested that cholera was spread by 'germs', although he was unsure what 'germs' actually were.

Bacteria

Scientists had known about bacteria ever since the invention of the microscope. In the late eighteenth century, a Danish scientist named Otto Müller had studied and described a number of different bacteria. In 1849, the French scientist Franz Pollender had noticed that bacteria were present in huge numbers in the blood of cattle which had died of anthrax. But doctors never imagined that these tiny, single-cell creatures could actually cause a disease that would kill a human being.

Louis Pasteur and the germ theory of disease

In the 1850s, Louis Pasteur was a French industrial chemist working on the fermentation of wines. Personal heartbreak – the death of two daughters from typhoid fever – led him to study disease. During the 1870s, Pasteur worked to establish that microbes were the cause of disease and he isolated several disease-causing germs. It is this which established him as one of the 'heroes of health' (see page 5) in early medical histories. Pasteur achieved cult status, particularly in France. One encyclopaedia describes the germ theory as 'probably the most important single medical discovery of all time'.

In 1864, Pasteur described the experiment in which – using a swan-necked flask – he claimed to have given the theory of spontaneous generation a 'mortal blow' by *proving* that decay was caused by dust and germs falling out of the air. When he boiled milk and left it in an open flask, the milk turned sour. Boiled milk kept in a swan-necked flask – into which germs could not fall – stayed fresh.

The importance of Pasteur

Recently, however, medical historians have questioned Pasteur's importance. Historians believe nowadays that Pasteur did not give ideas about miasmas and spontaneous generation a single 'mortal blow' as he claimed, but that they were 'gradually overturned' over a number of years.

In fact, Pasteur was not the first to claim that 'germs' caused disease, and it is arguable that the German doctor Robert Koch (see page 24-5) did more to establish that certain bacteria caused specific diseases. The germ theory in itself did not cure a single disease, and even doctors who accepted it could not really see how it was relevant to the way they treated their patients. Even in France, as late as 1879, the editor of the scholarly *Concours Médical* argued that, although Pasteur's work was 'a glimpse of the way ahead', it was by no means proven to be the only solution to the problem of disease: 'we should maintain a certain reserve for the time being and not see bacteria everywhere, after previously seeing them nowhere'.

Nevertheless, the idea that germs cause disease not only revolutionised surgery (see Chapter 5) and laid the basis for the revolutionary discovery of antibiotics in the twentieth century, it changed the way ordinary families behaved: when you wash your hands after going to the toilet, you do so because you know that 'germs cause disease'.

Pasteurisation

As part of his work on wine, Pasteur had discovered that heating the wine to 50°C killed the yeast which caused the fermentation, and stopped the wine going sour. This process came to be called 'pasteurisation'. Dairies in the USA and Scandinavia pioneered the practice of pasteurising milk: thereby killing the bacteria which caused tuberculosis, typhoid, diphtheria and dysentery. Pasteurisation is the process which ensures that the milk you drink is safe.

The key advances in public health and nursing (see Chapter 4) pre-dated the germ theory, and were based on what one historian has called 'the erroneous filth theory of disease' and the idea that it was morally important to be clean.

"CLEANLINESS IS NEXT TO GODLINESS."

Robert Koch and bacteriology

In 1879, Robert Koch, a District Medical officer for
Wollstein, near Berlin, took the germ theory of disease
to its next stage. It was one step to assert that germs
cause disease. The next step was to prove that a specific
germ caused a specific disease. In 1878, Koch actually
identified the germ which caused septicaemia
in wounds. He discovered how to 'stain' septicaemia
germs blue with the chemical dye methyl violet, and
how to photograph them. His assistant Julius Petri,
discovered how to grow 'cultures' of bacteria on a
substance made from potatoes and gelatine – now
called the 'petri dish' that school pupils still use in
their biology experiments today.

Medical researchers soon
realised that one man on his
own could not do the immense
amount of work needed to
discover all the germs that
cause disease, and they began
to build up research teams.
Huge medical institutes were
set up, with government and
private funding. The first –
shown here – was the Pasteur
Institute in Paris (1888).

Koch laid down the methodology of *how* researchers
should discover the germ that caused a specific
infectious disease. Even today his rules are called
'Koch's Postulates':
1. Make sure the germ is *always* present in every case.
2. Grow a pure culture of the germ.
3. Inject the germ into an animal to check that it
   contracts the disease.
4. The germ must be recovered from the infected animal.

The plague

In France, Pasteur and his students called themselves microbiologists; in Germany, Koch and his students called themselves 'bacteriologists'. There was tremendous rivalry between the two.

In 1894, plague broke out in Hong Kong. The first scientist to arrive there, in order to find out the cause of the disease, was a student of Koch, the Japanese researcher Shibasaburo Kitasato. He made friends with the English doctors there, and set up his equipment in the local hospital. Alexandre Yersin, a student of Pasteur, arrived slightly later, carrying his microscope in one hand and his steriliser in the other. He was forbidden to use the hospital, so he made friends with the local Catholic priest and set up a laboratory of his own.

Koch spent hours in his laboratory trying to identify the germs that caused particular diseases. In 1881, using a lantern and photographs, Koch showed his discoveries about the germ theory of disease to the International Medical Congress in London. Even Pasteur (who hated Germans) was forced to admit: 'This is great progress, Monsieur'.

Both men studied the blood and buboes (swellings) of infected patients and quickly discovered the culprit organism – a short stubby rod-bacterium, which was easy to stain with aniline dyes. Both men grew colonies of the bacterium on agar jelly, and both then injected it into animals to reproduce the disease. Both men then rushed their work into print. As a result of these findings, a Russian named Haffkine produced a vaccine during the Bombay epidemic in 1897. It was not very effective, however, and outbreaks of plague still occur.

Pathogens

Koch's work led to the discovery of many other pathogens (disease-causing bacteria). Koch himself identified the bacilli that cause tuberculosis (1882) and cholera (1883). The micro-organisms that caused diseases such as typhoid, tetanus, pneumonia, diphtheria, meningitis and leprosy were also discovered at this time.

Immunology

Pasteur and his team began to investigate inoculation. In 1880, they discovered how to vaccinate chickens against chicken cholera. In 1881, Pasteur discovered how to attenuate (weaken) the anthrax bacillus by heating it.

Pasteur had proved that he could inoculate animals, but what about human beings? In 1885, while he was developing an inoculation against rabies, an opportunity presented itself to find out: a 9-year-old boy called Joseph Meister had been bitten by a rabid dog. With nothing to lose, Pasteur inoculated the boy, who survived not only the dog bite, but also injection with a virulent form of the disease.

Pasteur knew that the Ukrainian zoologist Elie Metchnikoff, studying starfish, had investigated what he called 'innate immunity' – that the starfish's white blood cells (the 'phagocytes') seemed to be able to attack and ingest certain harmful microbes. In 1887, Pasteur brought Metchnikoff to a new laboratory at the Pasteur Institute to research how people might be given 'acquired immunity'.

With typical showmanship, Pasteur set up a demonstration of his anthrax vaccine at Pouilly-le-Fort, in France, using a flock of sheep. He inoculated 25 sheep and then, a fortnight later, gave anthrax to the whole flock. On 2 June 1881, Pasteur invited a group of journalists to witness – as he had predicted – the last un-inoculated sheep die, whilst 'the 25 inoculated animals frolicked and gave signs of perfect health'.

Is vaccination a dead end?

A number of successful vaccines were produced. In the 1890s, the British bacteriologist Almroth Wright produced vaccines against typhoid and pneumonia. Then, in 1906, two French microbiologists, Albert Calmette and Camille Guerin, developed the *Bacille Calmette-Guerin* (BCG) vaccine – which every school pupil is still given today to protect them against tuberculosis.

So was vaccination the solution to the problem of disease? It seemed that all that was needed was to take some dead or weakened germs, inject them into the patient, and let the body learn how to defend itself.

However, back in 1890, Robert Koch launched 'tuberculin', a vaccine for tuberculosis. It did not work. And, in the 1920s, many of the vaccines produced by Almroth Wright – supposedly able to combat boils, colds, flu, sore throats, upset stomachs, catarrh and cancer – turned out to be failures. Although some vaccinations were successful there were diseases that the human body could not resist.

School textbooks relate how the young French doctor Charles Chamberland – one of Pasteur's researchers – discovered immunisation when he injected some chickens with an old culture of germs. Although the story may be true, it over-simplifies the story of the development of immunology, which Pasteur and his team had been investigating for a number of years.

Anti-bodies

The Germans developed the ideas of the French. In 1890, Emil Behring and Shibasaburo Kitasato – two members of Koch's research team in Berlin – discovered that a diphtheria patient could recover if given the blood serum from animals which had recovered from the disease. They did not know it, but they were giving the patient anti-bodies able to combat the disease. By 1913, they had modified this into an 'anti-toxin' which could inoculate against the disease. Other serums followed that could treat tetanus, plague and cholera.

Tropical medicine

In the nineteenth century two factors led Europeans to take western medicine to the rest of the world. Firstly, they wanted to build up huge overseas empires and needed their administrators and soldiers to stay well. Secondly, missionaries wanted to take Christianity to the rest of the world and saw medicine as a way to win the hearts of the native people: after 1893, the Church Missionary Society taught medical courses as part of its missionary training. In 1876, the Scottish doctor Patrick Manson – who had worked for 23 years in the Far East – linked the disease elephantiasis to a nematode worm parasite. What was groundbreaking about this work was his study on the life-cycle of the worm, during which he discovered that the disease was transmitted by the common brown mosquito.

Manson thought that malaria might also be transmitted by an insect and in 1897 the British bacteriologist Ronald Ross identified the anopheles mosquito as the vector (carrier). Other tropical diseases were discovered to be similar: yellow fever (a virus transmitted by mosquitoes), sleeping sickness (the parasite *trypanosoma* transmitted by tsetse flies) and bilharzia (parasitical blood flukes transmitted by water snails).

In 1899, Patrick Manson founded the School of Tropical Medicine, in London.

Medicine and empire

Europeans often presented conquered populations as peoples ravaged by diseases such as malaria, sleeping sickness and plague, for whom the advent of western medicine was a blessing.

However, imperial administrations spent only a small proportion of their budget on health measures, and most of their energies were devoted to keeping the white colonists, rather than the native population, healthy. The Indian nationalist Mahatma Gandhi rejected all western medicine, seeing it as merely a means of control over the Indian people.

Yellow fever and the Panama Canal

In 1903, the United States acquired the Panama Canal Zone, and set aside $150 million to build a canal. In 1904, the first Americans arrived in Panama; by 1905, there was a yellow fever epidemic, and panic. Enter Colonel William Crawford Gorgas. He made all westerners use mosquito-nets, and sent his officials to destroy the mosquitoes. The vector (the *aëdes aegypti* mosquito) bred in small puddles of water which had collected in stones, thrown-out tin cans etc. Gorgas made it an offence – punishable by a $5 fine – to allow any such environment for the larvae. Then, having deprived the mosquitoes of their usual breeding places, Gorgas put out frying pans full of water to attract them; and tipped the water down a disinfected drain when they had laid their eggs. Local swamps were drained, and all ditches and pools covered with a layer of oil. By September 1906, the epidemic was over, and Gorgas boasted: 'I have rid Panama of yellow fever – after 400 years!'

Panama, 1905: Colonel William Gorgas looks for his enemy, the mosquito.

Chapter 4

How did public health improve?

Bradford in the early nineteenth century

In the nineteenth century, Bradford grew up as an industrial town producing woollen and worsted cloth. An increase in the birth rate, along with migration from elsewhere in the country, caused Bradford's population to grow from 13,624 in 1801 to 279,761 in 1901.

The massive increase in population overwhelmed the public health facilities (the town produced 90 million litres of effluent a day in 1874). Before 1862, most waste was simply dumped in the streets, and Bradford in the 1840s was a chaos of 'courts, yards and dingy

alleys with overflowing privies, open cesspits, pigsties and slaughterhouses and effluent-laden watercourses'. Bradford's woollen factories produced black, sulphurous smoke six days per week, making Bradford the most polluted town in England. The workers caught anthrax from spores in the raw wool, and deformities and chest diseases were common among children who worked in the dangerous, dust-filled factories.

Large numbers of the population were Irish immigrants, who crowded into the poorer areas of the town. In the Goit Side area of Bradford, for example,

Bradford lay in a natural valley with hills on three sides, and all the drains of the town flowed into the Bradford canal. The canal became so thick with waste and human excrement that it was possible to walk on the 'water' and in summer the canal occasionally caught fire. People who could not afford to buy their water at high prices from the private water company took their drinking water from the canal.

1,450 people lived in 230 houses, and shared 435 beds and 36 privies (giving an average of three persons per bed and 40 per privy).

In 1844, James Smith, the Health of Towns Commissioner, declared Bradford 'the dirtiest, filthiest and worst-regulated town in the kingdom'. There were regular outbreaks of cholera and typhoid, and the average infant death rate in Goit Side was 329 per thousand live births. Life expectancy in Bradford in 1837 was less than 19 years.

Public health improvements: local or central?

The conditions in Bradford were typical of urban conditions in many towns during the Industrial Revolution. They did not cause alarm for only medical reasons. Middle class campaigners were horrified by the poverty, alcoholism, ignorance and poor morals of the working classes in the poorest areas. Poor areas were also a breeding ground for crime, violence and revolution. Thus, a number of factors lay behind the movement to improve living conditions in the towns.

The situation in Bradford was typical of urban life in many industrial towns. This 1881 picture from the American magazine *Harper's Weekly* purports to show the conditions in New York during the cholera epidemics.

Public health

Until recently, historians represented advances in nineteenth century public health solely in terms of the laws passed by central government, and the actions of reformers such as Edwin Chadwick (see page 33). Central governments often conducted the investigations which provided the statistical and political justification for action, and much of the money for improvements came from central government grants and loans. Recently, historians have placed much more emphasis on civic pride and the work of local government in public health reforms, particularly the desire of many town councils to 'look good' compared to other towns (see page 36).

The hygienists

Public health (the work of governments in preventing disease) was not the invention of the late nineteenth century, or a product of the germ theory of disease. The miasma theory (see page 20) encouraged a 'hygienic' approach to the environment. In the eighteenth century many countries established 'medical police' (rules about hygiene, quarantine etc) and a number of British towns applied for Acts of Parliament which allowed them to appoint medical officers, build sewers, remove nuisances and drain local swamps. Even Bradford, in 1803, set up a Board of 'Commissioners' which set scavengers to collect waste, bought a fire engine, laid pavements, prosecuted pig-owners who let their sows run loose in the streets, and contracted with the Bradford Gaslight Company to erect lampposts. When the cholera epidemic of 1832 came to Bradford, the Commissioners set up a Board of Health and built a hospital with a subscription of £300.

Villermé investigated the damage modern industry did to the workers' health, including that of children (which led to the 1841 French Child Labour Law).

France: Louis René Villermé

Ideas about public hygiene developed in France during the Revolution. The new *écoles de santé* (see page 12) included a department of hygiene, which in the next half-century produced studies on sewerage, housing, water, industrial poisons, naval and military hygiene, gymnastics and child hygiene.

The most famous French hygienist was Louis René Villermé, who, in 1826, proved a statistical correlation between poor social conditions and high death rates.

'Filth and stench'

The pre-bacteriology hygienists fought a war against 'filth and stench'. Although their theory of disease was wrong, the public hygiene measures they took helped significantly to remove the environment in which disease flourished.

America: Lemuel Shattuck

Lemuel Shattuck was a teacher who became a publisher and politician. He persuaded the Massachusetts State Legislature to record births, marriages and deaths, and he designed the 1850 federal census. In 1849, he was appointed Chief Commissioner of a Sanitary Commission 'to prepare and report a plan for a sanitary survey of the State'. Shattuck's Report proved that in Massachusetts the poor died younger than the rich, and that most of the diseases they died from were preventable through basic hygiene.

Shattuck's recommendations, based on a study of public health provision abroad, became the basis for the Massachusetts Board of Health, the first Board of Health in America in 1869.

England: Edwin Chadwick

Chadwick was a barrister who was an expert on the Poor Laws. Instead of treating the symptoms of illness by giving people welfare, he tried to target the cause of disease by introducing public health measures. His *Report on the Sanitary Conditions of the Labouring Population of Great Britain* (1842) argued that the government could reduce expenditure on the poor if it spent money on public health.

The cholera epidemic of 1848–49 gave Chadwick the leverage he needed, and the Public Health Act of 1848 set up a central General Board of Health (with Chadwick in charge) with power to appoint medical officers of health, build sewers, clean streets and inspect food.

Edwin Chadwick's success was short-lived: when the cholera epidemic receded, he was dismissed (1854) and his Board of Health was abolished (1858).

Germany: Rudolf Virchow

Rudolf Virchow (see page 17) rose to fame in 1848 when the Prussian government asked him to investigate an outbreak of typhus in Silesia. He came to the conclusion that the main fault lay with a government that allowed people to live in poverty and squalor. Virchow became a life-long agitator for social reform. In 1859, he became a city councillor in Berlin, where he planned and oversaw the building of the new sewage system, two new hospitals and a school of nursing, and improved the water supply, meat inspection and school hygiene.

Florence Nightingale

One of the most prominent and influential hygienists of the nineteenth century was Florence Nightingale, who achieved fame for improving the standards of cleanliness in hospitals.

The Crimean War, which broke out in 1853, was a disaster. One military catastrophe of this war is commemorated in the poem 'The Charge of the Light Brigade'. Moreover, it was the first war to be extensively reported in the newspapers: William Russell from *The Times* was there to record each British and French setback as it happened.

At the time, Florence was Superintendent of the Institution for the Care of Sick Gentlewomen in Distressing Circumstances, in London. Desperate for some positive press, Sidney Herbert, Minister of War, asked Florence, in 1854, if she could go and help in the British Army hospital at Scutari, where wounded soldiers lay untreated and rotting along four miles of corridors. Florence Nightingale and her team of nurses scrubbed floors and nursed the wounded. After her

The romantic image of Florence Nightingale, 'the lady with the lamp', whose shadow the soldiers were said to have kissed. In reality, her linen Turkish lamp would not have thrown enough light to make a proper shadow!

How successful was Florence Nightingale?

Florence Nightingale's reputation was a creation of the newspapers. In reality, the death rate at Scutari while she was in charge was higher than any other hospital, and it was an army sanitation team that cleaned out the sewers and a French doctor who improved the food. She did not invent the idea of trained nurses (Theodore Fliedner had set up the Deaconess Institute in Germany in 1836, where Florence trained in 1851) and in fact the Nightingale School for Nurses she founded produced very few nurses. Provincial Nursing Associations in England did as much to promote professionalism in nursing as Florence Nightingale.

Nevertheless, though modern historians may debunk the actual achievements of Florence Nightingale herself, the principles popularised by the myth she inspired led to a radical improvement in the quality of hospital wards and nursing care throughout the world.

work was reported in *The Times*, she became famous as 'the lady with the lamp'. For the rest of her life she used her reputation and connections to support the development of a well-trained nursing profession.

Red Cross

In 1859, a Swiss businessman called Henry Dunant found himself wandering among the wounded after the battle of Solferino. The experience so horrified him that he set up the Red Cross to help the victims of war.

In America, Clara Barton – who hated being called the 'American Florence Nightingale' – had, similarly, started raising money to help the huge numbers of soldiers wounded in the American Civil War. In 1869 – in Switzerland to recuperate after illness – she met up with Red Cross officials, and in 1881 she formed the American Red Cross. It was Clara Barton who first mobilised the Red Cross for a natural calamity (the Michigan fires of 1881).

This photo of a hospital ward in New York, USA, shows a typical nursing ward of the early 1900s. Notice the high standards of hygiene and cleanliness, and the professional, uniformed nurses. The influence of army hospitals can be seen in the precise ranks of beds.

Local initiatives

After 1850, many cities introduced public health measures on a huge scale. By 1900, Paris had 692 miles (1,113 kilometres) of sewers. By 1895, every house in Hamburg and 95 per cent of houses in Berlin had running water. In 1885, the New York City Department of Health bacteriologically examined and destroyed 1,701 quarts (1,932 litres) of milk, 72,700 pounds (32,977 kilograms) of sweets, 5,700 pounds (2,585 kilograms) of cheese, and 4,100 pounds (1,860 kilograms) of coffee. Even Bradford tackled the public health problem, setting up a 38-acre (15 hectare) sewage-treatment plant in 1874.

Chicago water

Chicago offers a fascinating example of a city struggling with disease. Cholera struck every summer from 1849 to 1854. The problem was that the city got its water from a pipe stretching 46 metres (150 feet) into Lake Michigan, but the Chicago River (nicknamed 'Bubbly Creek' after the bubbles which came from the decaying waste lying on the bottom) discharged all the city's sewage into the lake, contaminating the water supply.

In 1851, the city set up its own waterworks (the first municipal waterworks in America) and extended the

Between 1856 and 1859, London workmen lay 842 kilometres of sewers and 20,921 kilometres of drains.

inlet pipe 600 feet (183 metres) into the lake, in order to get away from the pollution from the sewage: it was no use. In 1867, the city dug an underground tunnel to an inlet 2 miles (3 kilometres) into the lake: but this still did not work. In 1871, the city spent $3 million diverting most of the Chicago River into the Illinois and Michigan Canal. This didn't work either (the water in the canal flowed too slowly). In 1873, there was another cholera epidemic, and in the 1880s the death rate from typhoid hit 178 per thousand.

Chicago was hosting the World's Columbian Exposition of 1893, and did not like being known as 'typhoid fever city'. In 1892–1900, the city built the huge Sanitary and Ship Canal – 25 feet (8 metres) deep, 160 feet (49 metres) wide and 28 miles (45 kilometres) long. It was so huge and so deep that it literally made the Chicago River flow backwards.

However, Chicago's drinking water only became safe in 1906, when the water was chlorinated. In the years 1922–1939, four sewage treatment plants were built.

Government reforms

Towards the end of the century, governments became more willing to intervene, not only with specific health measures and regulations, but also through social legislation that benefited the disadvantaged sections of society. Germany introduced sickness insurance in 1883, and both Germany and France ran public information campaigns encouraging better child-care. The British government also introduced welfare reforms, including old age pensions (1908), sickness insurance and unemployment pay (1911).

The World's Columbian Exposition of 1893 was held in Chicago, despite the problem of typhoid.

Chapter 5

What were the advances in surgery?

Surgery in the 1840s

Robert Liston, professor of clinical surgery at University College London, was one of the most celebrated surgeons in Britain. He was ruthlessly self-confident and fast. 'Gentlemen, time me' he would shout as he wielded the knife with flamboyant gestures; his record for an amputation was 2 ½ minutes.

In Liston's day, the average post-operative death rate was 35 per cent (65 per cent for amputations at thigh level). Half the deaths from surgery were due to blood-poisoning. In one whirlwind Liston operation, not only did the patient die from post-operative gangrene, so did the assistant (whose fingers Liston cut off by accident), and so too did an onlooker, whose coat Liston accidentally slashed and who (thinking he had been cut) had a heart attack. It was the only operation in history with a 300 per cent mortality rate.

Liston died from hospital gangrene in 1847, after he nicked his own finger during an operation.

Amputation – an etching (1785) by the satirical cartoonist Thomas Rowlandson – shows the horror of an amputation at the end of the eighteenth century.

Historiography of surgery

An operation in France
c. 1900. Notice the
clean conditions and the
medical gowns of the doctor
and nurses.

Before the mid-eighteenth century, surgeons were
generally the 'poor relations' of the medical profession:
setting fractures, lancing boils and removing external
growths. By 1914, surgery was seen as a normal
solution for a wide range of medical problems, and
consultant surgeons were important and respected.

Early historians of medicine interpreted advances in
surgery as the result of the genius of the 'heroes of
medicine': laying stress upon the improvements in
technology and the individuals
who pioneered those
technologies. Modern historians,
however, suggest that many
more issues were involved. In
fact, new experimental surgical
procedures, such as ovariotomies
and Sim's Operation, and
improvements in professional
prestige *pre-dated* the
improvements in technology,
such as the advances in
anaesthesia and antiseptics.

Carl Ruge

A German doctor, Carl Ruge, made an important
breakthrough in cancer surgery when he
realised that – for certain cancers – less than
half the people doctors operated on turned out
to have cancer. In about 1878, he developed
the technique of biopsy – studying cells from
the patient to see if they were cancerous –
which has become the basis of all cancer
treatment today.

An operation before anaesthetics

Before the 1840s, surgeons did not use anaesthetics (though some had experimented with 'mesmerism' – hypnotism). So this is how the Victorian novelist Fanny Burney described her mastectomy in 1811. It does not make easy reading:

'When the dreadful steel was plunged into the breast – cutting through veins – arteries – flesh – nerves ... I began a scream that lasted un-intermittingly during the whole time of the incision ... I concluded the operation was over – Oh no! presently the terrible cutting was renewed – and worse than ever, to separate the bottom, the foundation of this dreadful gland from the parts to which it adhered ... Oh heaven! – I then felt the knife against the breast bone – scraping it!'

This painting shows William T.G. Moore, left, administering anaesthesia to Gilbert Abbot while Dr John Collins Warren removes a tumour from Abbot's neck.

The discovery of anaesthetics

Humphrey Davy had publicized the painkilling effects of nitrous oxide ('laughing gas'), in 1800. It was used for entertainment in music hall shows, but only in January 1845 did an American dentist called Horace Wells use it to extract a tooth at Massachusetts General Hospital.

Three years earlier, another American dentist, William E. Clarke, had pulled a tooth using a different chemical: ether. In March 1842, the American surgeon Dr Crawford Williamson Long used ether for an operation, and a public demonstration took place on the 16th October 1846, when the American surgeon Dr J.C. Warren removed a tumour from a man's neck.

Five days after Warren's operation, Oliver Wendell Holmes coined the term 'anaesthesics' for the painkillers. By the end of the year, Robert Liston in London had amputated a leg using ether (in typical flamboyant Liston style; it took him 25 seconds to saw off the leg).

After 1847, the Scots doctor James Simpson (who so hated the pain he caused patients that he almost gave up medicine) discovered chloroform, and in 1884 the surgeon Carl Koller used cocaine as a local anaesthetic.

Dr Crawford Williamson Long (with the knife) amputating a leg c. 1857. Notice the anaesthetist administering the ether soaked into a towel. Anaesthetics were dangerous – about 1 in every 10,000 patients died.

Acceptance of anaesthesia

Modern historians do not argue – as they did in the past – about who 'discovered' anaesthesia. Rather, they ask, why did it take surgeons so long to use substances which they had known about for 40 years? And why – even though his patient was unconscious – did Liston still operate so quickly?

It took surgeons a long time to accept anaesthesia. Some doctors believed that God *intended* patients to feel pain, and some even claimed that pain made the patients try harder. Anaesthesia only really became popular after John Snow gave chloroform to Queen Victoria during the birth of her son, in 1853.

Lister and antiseptics

In 1927, Dr John Leeson remembered starting as a
student in London, in 1871 – in the days before
surgeons understood about germs:

'I remember the house-surgeon in the theatre with his
threaded needles dangling from the front flap of his coat
… An operation was a dirty job and an outworn old
coat was a suitable garment! I see it now, faded with
age, stained with blood and spotted with pus.'

There was little excuse for this state of affairs. In
1847, the Hungarian surgeon Ignaz Semmelweiss had
made all the doctors on his childbirth ward disinfect
their hands in calcium chloride solution before they
attended their patients. Deaths from puerperal fever
after childbirth fell from 12 per cent to 1 per cent.
Then, in 1865 Joseph Lister, professor of Surgery at
Glasgow University, learned about Pasteur's theory of
germs. He used a carbolic acid spray to disinfect his
operations and the patients' wounds, and his post-

Anaesthetics allowed surgeons
to do much longer, much more
complicated operations inside
the human body. In 1881, the
German surgeon Theodor
Billroth (shown here)
successfully operated on a
patient's stomach.

operative mortality rate fell from 46 per cent to 15 per cent. Lister's 'antiseptic surgery' meant that – for the first time in history – patients could go into hospital to have an operation with the expectation that they would get better, instead of being fearful of disease.

As the century progressed, surgeons attempted ever more adventurous operations. They learned how to go into the body, cut out the affected part, and then repair the tissues (this is called 'resective surgery'). By the first decade of the twentieth century, surgeons were experimenting – sometimes successfully – with transplants of organs such as pancreases, testicles and ovaries.

Opposition to antiseptics

Early medical historians saw Lister as the founder of a new age. In fact, when he moved to King's College London, he generally met with a hostile reception. One lecturer had a standard joke, telling students who failed to shut the door to do so quickly, lest one of Mr Lister's germs comes in! Few doctors at that time believed in the germ theory. Surgeons did not like being told that they were causing their patients' deaths. The nurses, also, felt that Lister was implying that they were not keeping the wards clean.

Lister's carbolic spray soon fell out of use. By the 1880s, surgeons were developing instead 'aseptic surgery' – operating under sterile conditions. In 1890, the American surgeon William Halsted introduced the use of rubber gloves during surgery and, seven years later, German surgeons started using face masks.

Thyroid Gland

Oesophagus

The Swiss surgeon Theodor Kocher discovered that, when he removed the thyroid gland (pictured here), his patients fell ill. So, in 1883, he tried replacing it with thyroid tissue from another person: the first ever transplant.

Hospital beds

In the early nineteenth century, there were no operations which were specific to hospitals. Minor operations, such as tonsillectomies, continued to be done in people's homes and doctors' surgeries well into the twentieth century. However, the development of intricate and internal operations towards the end of the nineteenth century established the hospital as the place where you went to have an operation. In England, the number of hospital beds rose from only about 4,000 in 1800 to 113,000 in 1891.

Chapter 6

How did treatment improve?

The end of the old

Towards the end of the eighteenth century, doctors had begun to question treatments based on the theory of the four humours. French doctors led the way. In the 1800s, Pierre Louis – who became *Interne des Hôpitaux de Paris* (Resident Physician of the Hospitals of Paris) in 1823 – proved that bleeding patients did not cure pneumonia. Doctors began instead to investigate whether there were any drugs or chemicals that would cure or alleviate disease, including substances such as strychnine (a poison used as a stimulant), quinine (a drug which cured malaria), morphine and codeine (pain-killers).

Magic bullets

The work of Pasteur and Koch on germs further encouraged doctors to continue looking for cures. The German bacteriologist Paul Ehrlich (1854–1915) investigated the effects of chemical dyes – if certain dyes could

This picture from 1912 – entitled *Health and Disease in Deadly Combat* – shows, in a drop of blood, 'the wonderful white cells attacking, swallowing, killing, digesting the black parasites which mean disease'.

Flu pandemic

Despite all the developments in medicine in the nineteenth century, there was still little doctors could do when faced with infectious disease.

In 1918, American soldiers training in the US began to catch flu. From there it spread to France and to Spain – where people began to call it Spanish flu – and then all over the world. A fifth of the population of the world caught the Spanish flu, and more than 20 million people died of it. It was the worst pandemic of all time.

stain certain bacteria, perhaps there were dyes that could kill them? Only two were successful: methylene blue, which attacked the malaria parasite, and trypan red, which attacked *trypanosoma*, the parasite that caused sleeping sickness.

So, Ehrlich began to try other chemicals. In 1889, he set up a private laboratory and assembled a research team. In 1909, after thousands of tests, his assistant, Sahachiro Hata, at last discovered that chemical number 606 (an arsenic compound called salvarsan) cured syphilis. Chemical, so-called 'magic bullets', however, were hard to find, and no others were discovered until the 1930s.

In 1893, the Danish doctor Niels Finsen found that ultraviolet light killed the tuberculosis bacilli in skin lesions. Dozens of sanatoria opened in the Alps, where tuberculosis patients spent hours sunbathing in the fresh air. Famous patients who attended sanatoria included Robert Louis Stevenson (who wrote *Treasure Island* there), Indira Gandhi (who became Prime Minister of India) and the poet T.S. Eliot.

New technology

What about other modern discoveries, could they perhaps help patients? Doctors tried magnetism, and tortured their patients with electricity. They injected them with animal hormones and extracts of guinea pig and dogs' testicles. More successfully, by 1900, doctors had also started to use radium (discovered only two years earlier by Marie and Pierre Curie) in the treatment of cancer.

A medical profession

There were significant improvements in both the quality and popular perception of doctors during the nineteenth century.

The quality of education for doctors improved greatly during the century. Some universities established medical schools at this time, although many had already been established years before. Universities sponsored research and hospital practice, improved student discipline and set meaningful examinations. In America, in 1910, Abraham Flexner surveyed 157 different medical schools and found many of them unsatisfactory. Several schools were forced to close down simply because they were unable to afford the required

A LUCID INTERVAL.

In this *Punch* cartoon of 1891, the maid is telling the doctor: 'Well – he has been wandering a good deal in his mind. Early this morning I think I heard him say, 'what an old woman that doctor is!' – and I think that was about the last really rational remark he made'. The cartoon pokes fun at the doctor, but he appears to be concerned, smartly-dressed and well-to-do. There is none of the vicious hostility shown in the eighteenth century caricatures of Hogarth (see page 4) and Rowlandson (see page 38).

facilities. By the end of the nineteenth century, there were practitioners without university training still practising medicine, but they were regarded by everybody as being of low status.

A code of ethics

Better training was connected to an improvement in professional behaviour. The first book on medical ethics was published by Thomas Percival, in 1803. Many others followed, and ethics became an important part of every university course. The forerunner to the British Medical Association was founded in 1832, the American Medical Association in 1847 and the French Association *Générale de Médecins* in 1858. In Germany, doctors formed local associations called *Ärztekammer*. These associations encouraged doctors to meet socially and professionally, and some of them enforced codes of ethics. At the same time, learned journals such as *The Lancet* (1823) and, in America, the *Medical Repository* campaigned for better standards and transmitted new research to ordinary doctors.

Doctors in 1800 were widely criticised. This Thomas Rowlandson cartoon is called 'Medical Dispatch' or 'Doctor Doubledose Killing Two Birds with One Stone', and shows a doctor neglecting his patient while he flirts with her daughter.

Hospital medicine

In the 1970s, the medical historian Nicholas Jewson argued that the nineteenth century saw the replacement of the old 'bedside medicine' (which concentrated on how the disease would develop and relieving the symptoms) with 'hospital medicine' (which concentrated on the diagnosis and classification of the disease). This, he argued, may have helped the progress of medicine, but – particularly in the use of technical jargon – meant that the patient was treated as a 'case', rather than as a person.

Women doctors

In Europe, in the nineteenth century, women were forbidden to become doctors, and had to fight to enter this male-oriented profession. Women were not allowed to study to become doctors anywhere in Europe before the 1860s, and not in Belgium, Norway, Spain or Portugal until the 1880s. In Britain, Sophia Jex-Blake founded the London School of Medicine for Women in 1874, and the British Parliament allowed women to qualify as doctors in 1876.

By contrast, in America, many women were actively engaged in the medical profession in the nineteenth century. They worked as midwives (where they were preferred to male doctors), nurses and doctors. As the century progressed, women's medical colleges and women's hospitals were established: Dr Lucy Sewell, resident physician at the New England Hospital for Women, was Sophia Jex-Blake's inspiration. In 1900, there were 7,000 female doctors in America. The only other country that welcomed female doctors was Russia (which had more than 1,600 in 1913).

Sophia Jex-Blake: went to Edinburgh University after she was rejected by London University. She was obliged to take separate classes from the male students and – after she had passed the exams – the University would not grant her a degree, only a 'certificate of proficiency' (which would not have allowed her to practise as a doctor). In the end, she got a degree in Switzerland and her licence to practise medicine in Ireland.

Elizabeth Garrett: she attended classes in London hospitals, went to court to force the university to allow her to take the exam, and then acquired a licence from the Society of Apothecaries (which did not have rules excluding women). In 1866, she set up the St Mary's Dispensary for Women, and in 1873, managed to be admitted to the British Medical Association.

Women excluded

Historians used to present the acceptance of female doctors as a successful struggle by certain key female pioneers such as Elizabeth Blackwell, Elizabeth Garrett and Sophia Jex-Blake. Recently, however, this approach has been questioned. In fact, few women became doctors, and opposition remained fierce. As late as 1911, there were only 495 women on the Medical Register in Britain and there were only 138 women doctors in Germany, in 1913.

In America, women doctors were faced with increasing male sexism, which eventually drove them out of the profession. The Flexner Report of 1910 forced the small women's medical schools to close, and the American Medical Association did not admit women until 1915. The number of women doctors plummeted – although women were still allowed to work as nurses and assistants in medical laboratories, where they did not threaten men's control of the profession.

Modern feminist historians have pointed out that getting women into the medical profession involved more than changing a few rules: the whole structure of society – for example girls' education, parental attitudes and institutional sexism – worked against women becoming doctors, even when they were allowed to do so by the law.

Elizabeth Blackwell: obtained a medical degree in America, and set up the New York Infirmary for Indigent Women (1857). Returning to Britain, she was accepted onto the Medical Register in 1858.

The role of women

Women were said to be unsuitable for doctoring (or work of any kind) because, said the *Manual of Midwifery* (1828), they were 'subservient to reproduction' (their role was to produce children):

'Her destiny is to be united to a husband and to become a mother...Women are more liable to diseases than the other sex. The constitution is more feeble, peculiarly influenced by the mysterious process of reproduction'.

Doctors believed that over-exercise would divert energy from the womb, leading to sterility, sickness and hysteria (the word 'hysteria' comes from the Greek word meaning 'womb').

The Modern Physician

The book *The Modern Physician* (1910) by Dr Andrew
Wilson gives us an idea of what professional medicine
was like for ordinary people at the turn of the century.

Dr Wilson complains about the 'quacks' who flooded
the newspapers of the time with advertisements for
their 'so-called cures'. Then he lists the kind of drugs
'most likely to be of service in a household'. These
included a number of chemical substances – for
instance he tells us that sulphuric acid is a tonic,
arsenic in water can help skin diseases, and different
preparations of ammonia are useful for liver complaints,
neuralgia and nervous troubles. Other substances
patients were recommended to take included alcohol,
caffeine, cocaine, iron, mercury, saltpetre, opium,
rhubarb, creosote and extract of the thyroid gland.
(Most of these are more likely to harm than to heal.)

In this *Punch* cartoon from
1869, a doctor visits a
fashionable patient. She
says: 'Cod-liver oil! I couldn't
take such horrible stuff as
that'. He replies: 'Well, what
would you say to a cream and
orange liqueur?' Despite all
the advances in medicine,
general practitioners could do
very little to cure sickness,
and their role remained
primarily to alleviate the
symptoms and reassure
the patient.

Useful recipes

Dr Wilson's section on 'Useful Recipes' illustrates the
kinds of home-medicine that people might have used.
A starch poultice could be smeared on the crusts of skin
diseases. A burn could be dressed with a liniment made

from olive oil, belladonna and chloroform. There are lotions for eczema and ringworm, and a number of powders, pills and mixtures for chest and stomach complaints. One recipe for constipation was made of aloes, strychnine and soap, and a diarrhoea recipe was made of chalk powder, bicarbonate of soda, chloroform and peppermint water.

There is a long section on nursing, and a detailed chapter on 'cooking for invalids' – since 'in many cases invalids are more dependent on food than on medicine'. Wilson advises that cooks should be 'exquisitely clean' and that meals should be recently-prepared using fresh ingredients. The kind of meals he recommends for patients include chicken broth, fish omelette, stewed tripe, arrowroot pudding and oatmeal gruel.

It is significant that none of the 'recipes' are described as 'cures', and the reader is left with the impression that many patients will never get better. In 1910, doctors could make the patient comfortable and relieve some of the symptoms, but the body had to heal itself – or the person died or remained an invalid.

The Philadephia firm selling these quack remedies promised the public that 'brighter hours will come' with the use of their medicines, which included pulmonary syrup, itch ointment and a pile remedy.

A great invention in health?

Part of the improvement in health in the nineteenth century was nothing to do with medicine, but was due to changes in the way people lived. The invention of the rubber condom (thought to have taken place in America in the 1870s) was especially important for women's health. It stopped the spread of sexually transmitted diseases. Mostly, however, it prevented women having to suffer a life of frequent pregnancy and childbirth, which had weakened and killed many women.

The playwright George Bernard Shaw called the rubber condom the 'greatest invention of the nineteenth century.'

Untrained healers

The powerlessness of doctors against disease, and the fact that they were far too expensive for ordinary people anyway, led many people to turn to 'quacks' (untrained healers). In Britain, in 1854, it was estimated that there were 6,000 such men.

Some popular movements rejected professional medicine altogether. These theories sometimes appealed to the new 'scientific' ideas of the time. Franz Anton Mesmer (1734–1815) and his followers claimed to cure patients by 'mesmerism' (hypnotism).

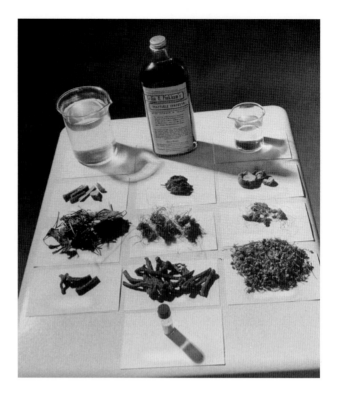

Similarly, Samuel Hahnemann of Vienna (1755–1843) held that infinitesimal doses of poisons and metals kept the body healthy – this idea was called homeopathy.

Most alternative medicines advocated personal hygiene and used 'natural cures' in some form or another. The American healer Samuel S. Thomson (1769–1843) advocated herbal cures, particularly the plant known as 'Indian tobacco', which caused vomiting and sweating. Vincent Priessnitz (1799–1851) of Vienna developed 'hydropathy' (water treatment), including vapour baths, brine baths and sulphur baths. Mary Baker Eddy (1821–1910), founder of the Christian Science religion, taught that the physical world –

Lydia E. Pinkham's Vegetable Compound – claiming to cure a range of female complaints from dizziness to the menopause – sold so well that 'Lilly the Pink' became America's first millionairess. This 1949 photo shows its ingredients: unicorn root, pleurisy root, black cohosh, fenugreek and a large amount of alcohol. It is now believed that black cohosh affects the serotonin (a chemical influencing mood) in the brain.

Alternative medicine

Many nineteenth century alternative medicines still survive today. Practitioners of 'Osteopathy' (the belief that the health of the body is affected by mechanical imbalances) and 'Chiropractic' (the manipulation of the spine to stay healthy) specialise today mainly in the treatment of back problems.

including disease and pain – was illusory. She advocated 'mind over matter' and the cure of 'disease' by faith alone.

The American Sylvester Graham (1795-1851) and his 'Grahamites' thought that sexual lust endangered health – he recommended hard mattresses, cold showers, vegetarianism and high fibre cereals. To this end he invented 'Graham Crackers' (a kind of digestive biscuit made from whole wheat flour).

Sequah, the great healer

The famous 'quack' William Henry Harley (known as 'the Great Seqah') worked in Britain from 1887–1895. Preceded by a brass band, dressed as a cowboy and surrounded by 'Red Indians', 'Sequah' would start by pulling out dozens of bad teeth at immense speed, much to the delight of the crowd. Then, after a short speech on the failures of modern medicine (while medical students shouted 'Science against quackery!'), he would sell his 'Prairie Flower Oil', a rheumatism cure supposedly made from herbs and mineral water found only in the Wild West (chemical analysis showed that it contained aloes, potash and alcohol). He was so successful that by 1890 there were 23 Sequahs working all over Britain and Ireland, and Sequah Ltd had been floated as a public company with a share capital four times that of Boots the Chemist.

In 1866, a religious group called the Seventh Day Adventists set up an alternative medicine 'Health Reform Institute' in Michigan. Their 'gospel of health' advocated a lifestyle based on hydropathy and roughage. In about 1894, as part of this regime, Will Keith Kellogg, brother of the Head of the Institute, rolled out a mash of maize and turned it into corn flakes.

Mental health in the nineteenth century

Before the nineteenth century, people with any mental illness or congenital disorder such as Down's Syndrome, were usually put together in a madhouse with alcoholics, syphilitics and the criminally insane.

However, during the French Revolution, Philippe Pinel – who had been put in charge of the Paris asylum – found that kindness and counselling could help mental health patients. In 1796, in England, a group of Quakers – outraged at the death through bad treatment of a Quaker patient in York asylum – set up the York Retreat, where 'neither chains nor corporal punishment are tolerated'. After a government commission (1816) found one patient in Bedlam asylum continuously chained to the wall by a leg-iron round his neck, there was a movement to treat the mentally ill more gently. A number of asylums were built where the ideal was 'moral management' – with treatments that included role play, occupational therapy, establishing a family-like atmosphere, and talking to the patients as though they were rational.

This treatment, however, still proved to be ineffective for many mentally ill patients. Investigators, such as ex-patient John Perceval (who formed the Alleged Lunatics' Friend Society in England, in 1845) and the

Hogarth's engraving of Bedlam asylum, based on an actual visit he made in c. 1735, gives an idea of how bizarre and often horrific such places were.

American social reformer Dorothea Dix (1802–1887), discovered that in many asylums mentally ill patients continued to be treated badly.

The development of psychiatry

In 1779, the Edinburgh doctor William Cullen had defined insanity, not as a disease, but as a nervous disorder originating in the brain. This was an important development, because – if mental illness was not a disease – it did not need treatment by doctors. In the nineteenth century, however, doctors began to claim the control of mental as well as physical illnesses. The German psychiatrist Wilhelm Griesinger (1817–1868) asserted that 'psychological diseases are diseases of the brain... insanity is only a symptom'.

As the century progressed, Benedict Morel (1809–1873) and Henry Maudsley (1835–1918) linked psychiatry with Darwin's ideas about evolution. Mental illness, they said, was 'degenerative' and linked to heredity or depraved behaviour (such as alcoholism or masturbation). The Italian criminologist Cesare Lombroso (1836–1909) linked degeneration to identifiable physical traits such as low brows and jutting jaws.

Franz Josef Gall (1758–1828) claimed that different mental faculties were located in different parts of the brain. His theory of phrenology (judging mental health by the lumps on the skull) is now discredited, but it was a very popular theory in the nineteenth century.

Mental illness

Treatments of mental illness in the later nineteenth century included straight-jackets, terror (such as whipping with nettles, submersing in a tub of eels and 'the whirling chair'), hypnotism and regression, cold shower-baths, removal (for women) of the womb or ovaries, lobotomy (after 1890) and increasingly, tranquilisers such as chloral hydrate and morphia.

Although treatments remained incredibly cruel long into the twentieth century, the gradual development of hospital care, and the attempts of doctors such as Sigmund Freud to try to understand and treat mental illness, nevertheless laid the foundations of modern psychiatry and mental health care.

Chapter 7

How successful was nineteenth century medicine?

Modern medicine

"Modern medicine, by which I mean 'our' medicine, was the product of nineteenth-century society", writes the medical historian W.F. Bynum, and it would be easy to represent the nineteenth century as a time of continuous and significant progress in the history of medicine.

The previous chapters have documented many fundamental medical advances: experimental physiology, cell theory, germ theory, bacteriology and immunisation, hygiene and public health, anaesthesia, antiseptics and nursing, and numerous advances in medical technology, from the stethoscope to the electrocardiograph. These developments turned out to be the essential foundations of the successes of medicine in the twentieth century.

Meanwhile, there was a parallel improvement in the skills and prestige of the medical profession. The respectable hospital consultant physicians of the early twentieth century were a world away from the doctors of the eighteenth century, who – as they fled London to get away from the plague – were stoned by the mob.

This painting, by the Victorian artist Luke Fildes, shows a doctor caringly but powerlessly watching a sick child.
A bottle of medicine and a cup sit useless on the table. The painting was inspired by Fildes's experience of the care shown by his own doctor for Fildes's son, Phillip.
This painting helped to improve the public perception of the medical profession, and many doctors hung a copy of it in their waiting rooms. In fact, poor people such as this family would never have been able to afford a proper doctor.

The 'heroes of health' of the nineteenth century are still famous today, and some of their names have entered our vocabulary – milk is said to be 'pasteurised' and you can buy an antiseptic mouthwash called 'Listerine'.

'A box of blanks'

Yet, for all the advances of the nineteenth century, doctors remained largely unable to cure disease. They carried, as the medical historian Roy Porter has called it, 'a box of blanks'. 'Had a [bubonic plague] epidemic occurred in western Europe at any time before 1939', comments the medical historian F.F. Cartwright, 'physicians would have been as helpless to cure their patients as were doctors in the Black Death'.

At the end of the nineteenth century, despite the advances in bacteriology and immunology, when faced with serious illness, doctors remained largely unable to cure infectious disease.

During the nineteenth century pharmaceutical firms grew up such as Bayer in Germany (1863) and Burroughs Wellcome & Co in America (1880). In 1898, Bayer invented a morphine-based cough syrup which they claimed would be non-addictive; they called it 'heroin'.

BAYER PHARMACEUTICAL PRODUCTS. Send for samples and Literature to FARBENFABRIKEN OF ELBERFELD CO. 40 STONE ST NEW YORK.

Deadly painkillers

Although painkillers are one of the greatest benefits of nineteenth century medicine, addiction was a terrible side-effect. The opium-based drug laudanum, used for headaches and to soothe crying babies, was freely available, and famous laudanum addicts included the poet Coleridge, the anti-slavery campaigner Wilberforce, King George IV of England and Wyatt Earp's wife, Mattie. Thousands of soldiers became addicted to morphine – another opium-based pain-killer – during the American Civil War.

In America, in 1886, a Dr John Stith Pemberton invented a soft drink, called Coca-Cola, to help morphine addicts quit – it was made from coca plants and cola nuts, and contained cocaine and caffeine.

Typhoid Mary

Despite the developments and inventions of the nineteenth century, disease was still a terrifying and sinister enemy. The case of 'typhoid Mary' illustrates just how vulnerable society was.

Mary Mallon in hospital. The doctors gave her urotopin – an antiseptic for the urinary tract – but, of course, it was useless; the antibiotics that could have cured her were not available for another 30 years.

Mary Mallon was an Irish immigrant in New York State who worked as a cook. She had eight jobs in seven years, and in seven of those families there were outbreaks of typhoid, a disease of the bowels (the bacterium which causes it, *salmonella typhi*, is passed on in food). In 1907, health officials tracked these outbreaks back to Mary – she had recovered from the disease, but was a carrier of the bacillus.

The idea of a 'carrier' was new in the 1900s and at first Mary was quarantined for two years in a hospital for communicable diseases. She complained that 'there was never any effort to do anything for

The syphonic flush toilet

A major advance in public health was the invention, in the late nineteenth century, of the syphonic flush toilet.

Thomas Crapper (1836–1910) had built up a successful plumbing business in Chelsea, and when the royal family refurbished Sandringham House in the 1880s, they installed Thomas Crapper toilets.

Thomas Crapper did not invent the syphonic flush toilet, and the slang word for faeces does not derive from his name (it is a medieval word). However, the hilarity his name caused during the First World War may have led visiting American troops to coin the American nickname 'the crapper' for the toilet.

me excepting to keep me a prisoner without being sick'. She was, she alleged, being kept there merely as 'a peep show for everybody'.

In 1910, Mary was released on condition that she never work as a cook again. She disappeared, and was only rediscovered in 1915, working as a cook at a women's hospital, when an outbreak of typhoid killed two of the patients there. Mary stayed unnoticed for so long because typhoid was such a common disease in the industrial towns and cities of the time.

Standards of living

Nevertheless, there is no doubt that – by looking at measures such as the death rate and life expectancy – people seem to have become healthier by the end of the nineteenth century. In 1976, Dr Thomas McKeown argued that this was due to improvements in the standard of living, and the benefits of facilities such as gas, electricity and plumbing. Although recently historians have argued that hospitals, and particularly public health measures, also played a part, it does seem that a wealthier population, better-fed and better educated in hygienic habits, was more able to avoid illness. Thus, in a way, the Industrial Revolution largely solved the health problems it created. The general improvement in health stemmed from a healthier environment rather than improvements in curative medicine.

The *real* improvements in curative medicine were waiting for the doctors and scientists of the twentieth century.

Just as important as the public hygiene measures of the nineteenth century was the gradual infiltration into the home of ideas about hygiene. Adverts encouraged housewives to buy products such as soap and disinfectants. In the 1880s, companies began to claim, not only that their products removed dirt and smells, but also that they killed germs.

Glossary

Acute infection a disease (e.g. a cold) which develops quickly but from which you can 'get better', as opposed to chronic illness.

Aetiology the investigation of the causes of diseases.

Amputation cutting off a diseased or damaged limb.

Anaesthetics pain-killers.

Anatomy the study of the structure and parts of the body.

Antibodies cells in the body which identify, attack and kill germs.

Antiseptics chemicals which kill germs.

Aseptic germ-free.

Asylum a 'place of safety', used for a place where mentally ill people were incarcerated.

Attenuated weakened.

Autopsy the dissection of a dead body, usually to establish the precise cause of death.

Bacilli (singular: bacillus) bacteria.

Bacteria Microscopic single-cell organisms lacking a nucleus, which can cause disease.

Bacteriologists the German term for researchers who study microbes.

Biopsy the removal of a small section of tissue from the body so that the cells can be studied in order to reach a diagnosis.

Cardio-vascular body systems associated with the heart and veins.

Carrier a person with an infectious disease (who may not demonstrate any symptoms) who infects others.

Chemotherapy treating diseases with drugs.

Chiropractic alternative theory of medicine which claimed to cure illnesses by manipulating the back.

Chronic illness a long-term condition (e.g. arthritis).

Congenital – a disease present at birth and usually (though not necessarily) genetic.

Degenerative in the sense it was used in nineteenth century medicine, this referred to any condition which doctors saw as a genetic deterioration to a less highly-evolved type.

Democracy a system where people elect their government.

Diagnosis the assessment of what illness a person has.

Electrocardiograph a machine which monitors the heart.

Endemic a disease which is continuously present in the population (e.g. tuberculosis)

Epidemic a sudden large-scale outbreak of a disease (e.g. cholera).

Ethics the moral code for a profession.

Eugenics a movement that wished to remove 'defective' or 'degenerative' genes from the human race, usually by sterilization.

Germ theory the theory that diseases are caused by germs.

Heredity where traits are handed down from one generation to the next in a person's genes.

Histology the visual study of cells to identify diseases and cancers.

Homeopathy alternative theory of medicine, which holds that taking poisons in tiny quantities preserves health.

Hormones chemical secretions from glands (e.g. thyroid, pituitary, adrenal, pancreas), which control how the body functions.

Humoral pathology the belief that health and the human body are controlled by the 'four humours' (blood, phlegm, yellow bile and black bile).

Hydropathy an alternative theory of medicine which advocates the use of water in health treatments.

Imbecile a nineteenth century word for a person with a low intelligence level.

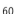

Immune system the body systems that resist diseases.

Inoculation an injection with a substance (usually an attenuated form of a disease) so that the body can gain immunity to that disease.

Kymograph a machine which measures the pulse.

Legislation the act or process of making laws.

Lobotomy an operation which severs the frontal lobes of the brain from the rest of the brain.

Lunatic a nineteenth century word for a person who is mentally ill.

Magic bullet Paul Ehrlich's term for antibodies.

Medical police an eighteenth century term denoting laws made to improve the public health.

Medicaments a nineteenth century word for medicines.

Menopause the time when a woman's body ceases to be able to have a baby.

Mesmerism a nineteenth century term for hypnotism, coined after its populariser, Friedrich Mesmer.

Miasma an eighteenth/nineteenth century term meaning a disease-bearing bad smell.

Microbiologists the French term for researchers who study microbes.

Midwives women who attend at childbirth.

Mortality rate death rate.

Obstetrics area of medicine concerned with pregnancy and childbirth.

Osteopathy alternative theory of medicine which claimed to cure illnesses by manipulating the bones, especially the back.

Pandemic an epidemic which spreads through a number of countries.

Parasite a plant or animal which lives on another organism, usually causing disease or the death of the host.

Pasteurisation the process of heating a liquid (e.g. milk) to kill the germs so that it lasts longer before it 'goes off'.

Pathology the study of what causes diseases and how this affects the human body.

Phagocyte a type of white blood cell which can engulf and destroy a germ inside the body.

Phrenology a system, now discredited, which held that the shape of the skull allowed doctors to diagnose mental traits and illnesses.

Physiology the study of how the body works.

Psychology the study of human behaviour, particularly insanity and mental health.

Public health the measures taken by the government to control health and disease.

Quacks unregistered healers (and, by implication, charlatans).

Quarantine isolation of people who have, or are suspected of having, an infectious disease.

Reductionism the idea that the human body is merely a series of physical and chemical reactions and involves no special 'spirit' or 'soul'.

Resective surgery cutting out part of the body, then repairing the remaining tissues.

Sanatorium an institution for the treatment of invalids and the chronically ill (tuberculosis patients).

Sanitation a system of drains, sewers and water pipes.

Scavengers people employed in the nineteenth century to collect refuse and sewage.

Socialism a political theory which believes that the state should own all the means of production, and use them for the benefit of all people equally in a classless society.

Spontaneous generation the erroneous pre-Pasteur theory that disease created bacteria (whereas today we know that the opposite is true).

Surgery medical operations on patients.

Vaccination a term, coined by Pasteur in honour of Jenner, meaning inoculation.

Variolation the procedure, common before 1800, of infecting children with a weak form of smallpox in the hope that they would gain immunity to the disease.

Vitamin an organic compound essential for the normal functioning of the body.

Vivisection the dissection of an animal or human being while they are still alive.

Timeline

Breakthrough dates in the history of nineteenth century medicine

Events	Dates	People
	1790	1796 Edward Jenner demonstrates vaccination for smallpox.
	1800	1803 Thomas Percival publishes his book on medical ethics.
	1820	1826 Joseph Jackson Lister invents the achromatic microscope lens.
		1829 Louis Villermé introduces statistical methods into public health research.
		1834 Pierre Louis suggests that changes inside the body are more important in diagnosis than outward symptoms.
		1839 Theodor Schwann shows that all tissue is comprised of cells, not humours.
	1840	1842 Crawford Williamson Long uses ether as an anaesthetic in surgery.
1847 Reductionism: German doctors declare that the processes of the human body are merely chemical reactions		1848 Edwin Chadwick sets up the first Board of Health.
		1854 John Snow disconnects the Broad Street pump, proving that cholera is not caused by a miasma.
	1860	1863 Henri Dunant sets up the Red Cross.
1876 An Act of Parliament allows women to qualify as doctors in Britain.		1867 Joseph Lister's research on antiseptic surgery is published in *The Lancet*.
	1880	1882 Robert Koch demonstrates the tuberculosis bacillus before the Berlin Physiological Society.
	1900	1895 Wilhelm Röntgen discovers X-rays.
		1902 Starling and Bayliss discover the first hormone.
		1906 Calmette and Guerin develop the BCG vaccine against tuberculosis.
1910 In America, the Flexner Report establishes the standards for schools of medicine.	1910	1909 Paul Ehrlich's team develop Salvarsan 606 as a cure for syphilis

Further information

Books

Philip Gates, *Medicine News* (Walker, 2001)

Gael Jennings, *Sick As: Bloody Moments in the History of Medicine* (Roland Harvey Books, 2000)

Nick Arnold, *Deadly Diseases* (Scholastic Hippo Horrible Science, 2000)

Ian Dawson and Ian Coulson, *Medicine and Health through Time* (Hodder Murray, 1996)

Schools Council History 13-16, *Project Team, Book 3 The Medical Revolution* (Holmes McDougall Medicine Through Time, 1976)

Neil Tonge and Michael Quincey, *Cholera and Public Health* (Macmillan History in Depth, 1985)

A Delgado, *A Hundred Years of Medical Care* (Longman, 1974)

Roy Porter, *Blood and Guts: A Short History of Medicine* (Penguin, 2003)

N Longmate, *Alive and Well: Medicine and Public Health from 1830 to the Present Day* (Penguin, 1970)

Roy Porter, *Quacks: Fakers & Charlatans in English Medicine* (Tempus, 2000)

James H Cassedy, *Medicine in America: A Short History* (John Hopkins University Press, 1991)

Roy Porter (editor), *The Cambridge Illustrated History of Medicine* (Cambridge, 1990)

Websites

http://www.bbc.co.uk/history/discovery/medicine/
A simple site which deals with advances in medicine, Florence Nightingale, and the battle against smallpox.

http://www.historylearningsite.co.uk/history_of_medicine.htm
Clear, informative school-pupils' site by Christine Truman of Sackville School, Sussex.

http://www.schoolshistory.org.uk/infectiousdisease.htm
A basic-information school-pupils' site which offers a hyperlink way through the subject.

http://www.historyworld.net/
A collection of illustrated timelines on Birth, Death, Drugs, Hospitals, Plagues, Surgery and Technology. Go through the Existing Timelines link, or enter 'Medicine through time' into the Index Search.

http://wwwihm.nlm.nih.gov/
Gateway to the US National Library of Medicine Images from the History of Medicine. Nearly 60,000 images of portraits, pictures of institutions, caricatures, scenes, and graphic art in a variety of media, illustrating the social and historical aspects of medicine, which you can browse or search by keyword.

http://www.library.ucla.edu/libraries/biomed/his/painexhibit/
Academic but clear site about anaesthesia.

http://www.healthsystem.virginia.edu/internet/library/historical/artifacts/caricatures/
An amusing site with nineteenth century cartoons, many of them about health and medicine.

http://www.whonamedit.com/
A detailed encyclopaedia of medical people.

Places to visit

The Old Operating Theatre
9a St Thomas's Street, London SE1 9RY.
Visit the website at
http://www.thegarret.org.uk/index.htm

Florence Nightingale Museum
St Thomas' Hospital, 2 Lambeth Palace Road, London SE1
Visit the website at http://www.florence-nightingale.co.uk/

For more information about places to visit:
http://www.medicalmuseums.org/

Index